TOU
BY GRACE

Walking the path of grief

WARREN R. BARDSLEY

CHURCH IN THE MARKET PLACE
PUBLICATIONS, *WARRINGTON*
2005
Second Edition 2008

British Library Cataloguing in Publication Data

A record for this book is available from the British Library

ISBN 1 899147 49 7

CHURCH IN THE MARKET PLACE PUBLICATIONS,
Warrington WA2 0LY

Typeset in Monotype Baskerville by
Patricia Saunders, Godmanchester

Printed in Great Britain by
Ralph Wrightsons Ltd, Earls Barton

TOUCHED
BY GRACE

*To my family
with love*

Contents

Prefaces

On 7 January 2004, my wife Joan died in the intensive care unit of the Royal Worcester Hospital. She was just over seventy and we had been married for forty-one years. In that moment life changed forever. In my pre-Christmas letter to family and friends this year, I used the phrase, 'strangely and wonderfully touched by grace' to describe my journey during the ensuing months. Over that period, I kept a daily diary, not with any thought of publication but as a way of setting down my feelings about what was happening to me.

For myself – though I know it will not necessarily be the same for others – this has been therapeutic. Soon after the first anniversary of Joan's death, it occurred to me that there might be those for whom the account of my journey could prove helpful. I know how much comfort I have found in the spoken and written words of others.

Of course, I am aware that in one sense, my story is not unusual. Thousands of people lose loved ones by death every year, some in tragic circumstances, and no two people mourn in exactly the same way. Nevertheless, there are common threads running through this devastating human experience; there is, I believe, a fellowship of grieving.

I trust that those who read these pages will find that which resonates with their own pain and discover as I have done, that the dark valley *can* be a place of growth – truly touched by grace.

WARREN R. BARDSLEY
Lichfield, Easter 2005

Preface to Second Edition

It was some words by the American psychologist, Carl Rogers which finally decided me to publish this book in March 2005. I had hesitated for several weeks, mainly because I wondered if an experience which was so deeply personal could possibly be relevant to anyone else. Rogers said: "What is most personal and unique in each of us, is probably the very element, which would, if it were shared and expressed speak most deeply to others'. This has been amply confirmed in the response to 'Touched by Grace'. I have been surprised and humbled that so many have been helped by the book and I'm deeply grateful for those who have been kind enough to write and tell me.

I am especially grateful to Lady Grace Sheppard, who encouraged me to believe that a reprint was not only desirable but essential, and who so readily and generously agreed to write a foreword to this edition. It remains true that there is no subsititute for personal recommendation; I am indebted in this regard to several friends and to Donald Eadie, in particular, through whose commendation the book has reached a number of folk who might not otherwise have heard about it.

January 2008

Acknowledgements

I would like to thank those who through their love and prayers have been channels of God's grace to me on this journey.

I am grateful for permission to use copyright material. The poem 'No Time' by R. S. Thomas, on page 20, is reproduced by kind permission of the publisher and is taken from *Collected Later Poems by R. S. Thomas (1988–2000)*, Bloodaxe Books, 2004. The extract from *The Lovely Bones* by Alice Sebold, on page 46, is used with the permission of Picador UK.

My thanks also to Bob Davies and his team at Church in the Market Place Publications for their encouragement and professionalism in the publication of this book.

The decorative motifs at the beginning and end of each chapter were designed and used by Joan.

Foreword

by Lady Grace Sheppard

To lose someone we love is our ultimate dread. It was certainly mine. There is no way of knowing how we will take the blow or manage our loss. For some it is a pain that never goes away. For others letting go happens bit by bit, until the cloud of grief gives way to sunshine and the will to move on is stirred. Everyone is different.

One thing however we share and that is our humanity. We laugh. We cry. We hurt and we heal. For a Christian there are certain expectations that we will cope better than most when losing a loved one because of our faith. But if we race to Easter without acknowledging the Good Friday experience this can cloud our humanity sometimes, and we fail to feel the pain. Even the joy may sometimes feel phoney. Bereavement cannot be rushed. There is no quick fix.

Honesty for a Christian is the beginning of freedom. This is what I love about **Touched by Grace.** Warren Bardsley has been generous enough to share his experience of losing his beloved wife with a refreshing openness and courage and a remarkable dignity. He spoke to my condition. As a Methodist minister, he demonstrates that he is very human. To walk with him in this treasure of a book is indeed to be touched by grace. His choice of quotations hits the spot again and again. He also draws strength from the spiritual legacy that his wife Joan has left him.

While there is a temptation to throw a book at someone who is grieving, it should be done with sensitivity. The concentration is not always there. An old friend who knew me well gave me a copy. This book is a little book, easy to handle, easy to read and easy to digest. But it is also a great book and one which I found such a help in my own journey of bereavement. Warren Bardsley's honesty and humanity refreshes the spirit and everyone should have a spare copy in the house to pass to a friend when the time feels right, having read it first.

GRACE SHEPPARD
Wirral 2008

Introduction

When we gathered as a family to celebrate Joan's seventieth birthday early in September 2003, we had no idea that it would be for the last time. She had a 'thing' about her age – perhaps because she was some years older than me, though she actually looked considerably younger! So, I was delighted when she agreed that her seventieth was an event worth celebrating, and we had a memorably happy day together.

In less than a month, she was in hospital with suspected pericarditis, where heavy doses of antibiotics and steroids seemed to be successfully fighting the infection. After three weeks she came home in an extremely weak condition but gradually, with support from local health and rehabilitation services, appeared to be regaining strength.

Then in early December the original symptoms returned with greater severity. Back in hospital, there followed two weeks of further tests and various invasive procedures. When, four days before Christmas, it became clear that her condition was deteriorating, she was sedated, ventilated and transferred to the intensive care unit at Selly Oak Hospital, Birmingham.

On Christmas Eve she returned to Worcester, and although she regained consciousness and seemed at one point to be making something of a recovery, she suffered a massive heart attack and died on the evening of 7 January. The underlying cause of her illness still remains something of a mystery.

The day of Joan's funeral was fixed for 20 January and, following a private cremation in Worcester, we met at Green Lane Methodist Church Leominster for a service of thanksgiving. We had lived and served together in the Leominster circuit during the 1980s; we still had a number of good friends there, and often returned to visit. The service was sensitively led by the local minister, Andrew Deans, and Anne Greet, minister at Worcester, who had been a caring pastor to us both.

Somehow I found the strength to pay my own tribute. I spoke of Joan's growing up in Northern Ireland and her call to serve God in the Wesley Deaconess Order; of our meeting and falling in love during a student mission in Liverpool, our partnership in ministry in Sierra Leone and half a dozen English circuits. I spoke of her warm and gracious personality; her honesty; her creative imagination; her ability to understand and get alongside all kinds of people; her sensitivity and vulnerability and above all of her capacity for love. We remembered her Irish roots and the renewal of her faith in a rediscovery of the Celtic vision. We played a recorded version of St Patrick's Breastplate and sang the ancient Irish hymn 'Be thou my vision'.

Our two sons, John and Richard, spoke movingly of their Mum and her influence on their lives, and we were comforted by the large number of friends who gathered to remember Joan and give thanks with us.

Someone has said; 'The funeral is the last thing you can do for a loved one. It is important to do it well.' I felt that she would have approved. As John and Richard remarked afterwards: 'We did her proud.'

In my address I spoke of dark and difficult days ahead. Just how dark and difficult these were to be, I was soon to discover.

I

Death

'Death is nothing at all ...' ?

CANON SCOTT HOLLAND

We were a couple;
now uncoupled.
A pair;
now impaired.
Joined together;
now disjointed.

☙☙☙

During a ministry spanning forty years I have conducted hundreds of funerals in all kinds of circumstances. In those situations I have tried to be a comfort
to loved ones and friends caught up in the experience
of bereavement. I have used the words of Scott
Holland on numerous occasions. They say something
important about the continuity between life on earth
and the life of the world to come. I know, from letters
received that they have touched the need of grieving

relatives. However, I wish that I had taken the trouble more often to make the point that the words imagine the dead person speaking from the other side. Otherwise, the opening sentence can sound false and unfeeling. I was reminded of this when reading Sheila Hancock's account of her life with John Thaw, *The Two of Us*, in which she describes her reaction to the words following John's death.

> Nothing helps. Especially that 'death is nothing at all' bollocks. Oh, really? And no, he isn't in the sodding next room. The thoughtful strangers say it will help me but it makes me roar with rage. He is utterly gone and I can't bear it.

This is the immediate reality. I wrote in my diary that her death feels like an amputation, a dismembering – as if a major part of you has gone, and, like the phantom limb, you keep feeling for it as though it is still there. Of course, it isn't. So to say that death is nothing at all … 'a negligible accident', without qualification is patently untrue. For those left to grieve it is undoubtedly *something* – something momentous, devastating, shocking. It *feels* absolutely final. After this moment life can never be the same again, and although you are assured that 'time will heal' you can't imagine *then* that the pain won't go on indefinitely. You are wounded, bleeding inside, ploughed up, torn apart. Whatever words are used to describe it, the experience is sheer hell and if the essence of hell is separation, the metaphor is wholly appropriate.

The first and overwhelming sensation, which to some extent is still there, is of physical absence. This is not simply or even mainly about sex. It is about a shared intimacy, touching, hugging, holding hands. This physical deprivation was deeply painful. I would wake up sometimes in the middle of the night, aching for her, crying out for her touch. I think I understand now, why some people who have enjoyed a long and happy married life remarry so quickly following a bereavement. I also understand the need to make contact with the beloved person, which may lead some to dabble in spiritualism and seek the help of mediums. Although I have done neither – and strongly advise against the latter – I can sympathise with those who do. The agony is acute, and an important part of the grieving process is facing up to this pain of separation. Sometimes the only way you can survive is to hang on.

Travelling in Ireland you may come across those peculiar round 'pencil' towers and wonder why the door is more than halfway up the outside wall. It was there for a very good reason. When raiders were approaching, members of the community would use a ladder to climb on to the platform just inside the door. Then when everyone was safely inside, the ladder was drawn up, the door secured and the people would remain there until the enemy forces had passed through. Just hanging on, believing that 'this too will pass'.

Leaving

You left
quite suddenly.
Tired of the waiting.
Tired of the
postponements and
cancellations.
Tired of the body's
harsh dictation to
the spirit.
And as the train
disappeared far into
the distance
I was left standing
on the platform …
Alone.

2

Doubt

Christ be beside us as we grieve
Daring to doubt or to believe.

JOHN BELL

☙☙☙

People give you all kinds of seemingly strange advice in the early stages of bereavement. 'Eat plenty' and 'keep warm', are just two examples of those offered to me. Curious, until you realise that the shock of separation has physical as well as emotional repercussions. For almost a year after Joan's death, I suffered intermittent bouts of chronic indigestion and abdominal discomfort, which I attributed to the effect of raw grief reacting on the body.

I was determined not to succumb to self-pity. I know from pastoral experience how corrosive it can be. Of course it is natural to feel sorry for yourself when a beloved partner dies, but that is quite different from *wallowing* in self-pity.

The story is told of Bishop James Pike that when

he and his wife were travelling in the Middle East they stopped their car in the Judean wilderness in order to spend some time looking around. He walked too far, lost his bearings and perished in that inhospitable desert. To dwell in the wilderness of self-pity not only robs us of the resources we need to *cope* with our troubles but can ultimately destroy us. A wilderness is a place to pass *through*, not a permanent home.

Unexpectedly, I found myself assailed by *doubt*. Not doubt in the existence of God, but in the continuing existence of Joan. I had written to friends following the funeral: 'Never have I been so sure of the truth of the resurrection.' I quoted those words by Richard Baxter, which he had penned following his own wife's death:

> In spirit we each other greet
> And shall again each other see.

Now, I found myself questioning this affirmation – one which I had so often and with so much confidence shared with bereaved people in pastoral conversation; the conviction that their loved one and friend was not in limbo, wandering in some shadowy existence, but secure in the love of God, and more fully alive than ever before. Moreover, I would share my conviction about the hope of re-union. Suddenly, as if being questioned by some invisible inquisitor, I was confronted by doubt and uncertainty: 'Do you really believe this? Is she truly still alive? Is the life of the world to come a reality or an illusion?'

I found myself, almost in a panic, clutching at straws, turning to books, looking for arguments to re-assure me. Deep down I was craving *evidence* of Joan's continuing existence and of course finding none. This is where grief can play strange tricks on the mind. I know the difference between faith and feeling, and have often spoken about it; the truth that faith is not in the genes but is a matter of choice and commitment. Now, that faith was being severely tested. Other questions kept hammering on the door of my mind: Why did she have to suffer so much during those final weeks of her life? Why did she have to die *now*, when she seemed to have so much to look forward to?

This questioning became quite irrational. Could she not have lived to see another Christmas? Survived to see her grandchild? Not only did I feel anger towards God, but angry with *her* for leaving! Then I would be overwhelmed by guilt for thinking this way. I couldn't bear the thought that I would never hear her *voice* again. I searched frantically and fruitlessly for her relaxation tape. Linked to all this was a sense of fear about the future. Would I be able to cope? The questions gnawed at me and refused to be silenced.

There is a type of doubt which is essential to faith – a questioning which is the necessary condition for faith's growth. *This* questioning was of a different kind. It was a disabling, paralysing doubt which seemed to be undermining the very foundations of faith.

I shared some of this agony with Bob, an ex-colleague whose own wife had died a number of years previously. He spoke of his own strong belief in the resurrection and his certainty that in Christ, separation from those we love is provisional.

'How can you be so sure?' I pressed him. He replied, 'Its a matter of TRUST. I have trusted Christ for life and he has been true. So when he promises that he has gone to prepare a place, why should I not trust him also for death and what lies beyond?'

Over the weeks which followed I realised that this meeting was a key moment in my journey through grief. God was graciously leading me to a deeper trust, not in a set of propositions but in *himself*.

During this confused time, I found myself living in the Psalms. I reread a little book by the Old Testament scholar, Walter Brueggemann, in which he describes the pattern found in many of these ancient songs. There is the journey from orientation, through dis-orientation to re-orientation, which he graphically describes as the movement from the 'pit' to the 'wing'. I knew that I was in that place of dis-orientation – the pit – but I clung to the hope that I would move to the place of re-orientation and find wings again. 'Hope in God, *for I shall yet praise him*' (Psalm 42:11).

Around this time I wrote a poem called 'Asking the right question', which expressed something of what I was feeling:

> Why?
> Why did she need to suffer
> so much
> at the end?
> This question has haunted me.
> Why the indignity of
> total dependence on
> strangers,
> robbed of speech,
> helpless?
> Why?
> No easy answer.
> I do not believe in a God
> who inflicts this
> humiliation.
> He is no monster.
> Then someone said:
> 'During those weeks
> she knew as never
> before how much
> you loved her.'

Not an answer, but
perhaps *why?* is the
wrong question.
Maybe *how?*
is better.
And in the end
the only real answer
is love.

3

Birth

... wherever you go I will meet you
Till you draw your last breath in the birthplace
    known as death ...
Saying 'Here am I'.

WILD GOOSE WORSHIP GROUP

☙☙☙

Gabriel was born in the dying hours of 1 April, even though his parents had hoped that he would hang on for a little while longer! He is the firstborn of our younger son, Richard, and his wife, Natalie. During her first spell in hospital Joan had said to one of her doctors: 'You must get me better. I'm expecting a new grandchild next year!' When the maternity ward rang around 10.30, I instinctively turned to her to share the good news. Later, when through my tears I rang the hospital with my congratulations, I realised again how closely joy and pain are woven together.

Next day as I held our latest grandson in my arms,

I felt Joan very close and when, weeks later, he smiled at me for the first time I had an indescribable, mysterious sense of recognising her behind the smile. I gave him a blessing:

> May you give and receive love;
> may you trust and be trusted;
> may you dare and be daring;
> may you be happy and bring happiness;
> and may you walk in God's sunlight all your days.

Three days later I received news of the death of a former colleague who had been fighting cancer. It led me to reflect again on the mystery of death and birth. On St Patrick's Day we had planted a young oak tree in memory of Joan. She was a gardener and enjoyed growing things, so it seemed fitting that this lovely area of parkland adjoining a crematorium should be the place where we can go from time to time to remember her. When we planted the tree we recalled the words of Paul in 1 Corinthians 15:

> The seed you sow does not come to life unless it
> has first died ... sown in humiliation it is raised
> in glory; sown in weakness it is raised in power;
> sown a physical body it is raised a spiritual body.

In a sense, birth itself is a sort of death. Hard though it is to imagine the life of a baby in the mother's womb, we may assume that it is a state of warmth and security. Imagine if we were able to ask the growing individual about the possibility of leaving behind this cosy state, to be launched into a completely new and unknown level of being, called life on earth. The chances are that he would opt to settle for the *status quo*! Purely speculative of course, because all the forces within the mother are preparing the baby for the moment of that traumatic exit through the birth canal. To live he has to leave behind the security of the womb. To experience the wonder of life in *this* world he has to abandon that state of total dependence. The analogy breaks down, of course because the baby doesn't *have* a choice. Our progress through life *after* birth, however, *is* a series of choices, and some of the important ones are about dying, and letting go.

The parent saying goodbye to her child at the school gates for the first time; the adolescent leaving school; moving house; the transition to old age; these are what someone has called 'times of the little death', preparing us in a sense for the great moment, when by the grace of God we will come to the final birthplace, and discover the wonder of that new world. Paul describes it thus:

> things beyond our seeing, things beyond our hearing, things beyond our imagining, all prepared by God for those who love him.
>
> 1 Corinthians 2:9

Malcolm Muggeridge, when travelling in Ireland with his friend Alec Vidler, came across an old woman sitting outside her cottage, who told them that she was learning how to die. Far from being morbid, this is a large part of the art of living. There are so many people who are not truly alive because they haven't learned how to leave behind false securities and move forward to embrace the new.

To say that I was longing for Easter 2004 is no exaggeration. Easter, apart from its central importance for every Christian, had a further significance for Joan and myself. We met at Easter, and two years later we got engaged in Easter week. It had always been a special time for us.

I got up early on Easter day and drove through the darkness to the Malverns where we had often rambled together. I watched the dawn break slowly over the hills, quietly read the Easter gospel, then walked for a while. The silence and peace, punctuated only by the song of birds was incredible.

I was frequently close to tears in the morning service at St Andrews Worcester, especially in the singing of the great Easter hymns. Joining members of the congregation as they carried flowers to adorn the cross, brought back sharp memories of Joan, who had shared on several occasions in this simple and powerful liturgy in which the tree of pain and death is transformed by the love of God in the rising of Christ from the grave. Later, receiving the bread and wine, I truly *heard* the word of promise:

> God gave us new birth into a living hope by the resurrection of Jesus Christ from the dead, the hope of an inheritance, reserved in heaven for you which nothing can destroy or spoil or wither. This is cause for great joy ...
>
> 1 Peter 1.3–4

Travelling home after the service, I thought of the words of A. E. Whitham: 'All too good *not* to be true'!

4

Severe Mercy

… impalpable,
invisible, she comes
to me still, as she would
do, and I at my reading.
There is a tremor
of light, as of a bird crossing
the sun's path and I look
up in recognition
of a *presence in absence*.
Not a word, not a sound,
as she goes her way,
but a scent lingering
which is that of time immolating
itself in love's fire.

R. S. THOMAS, 'No Time'
(my italics)

One way or another, the thing had to die.
Perpetual springtime is not allowed … you have
been treated with a severe mercy.

C. S. LEWIS *to Sheldon Vanauken*

A few weeks after Joan died I went to see her consul-
tant. I had requested the appointment, following the
inconclusive nature of the post-mortem and inquest.
He generously gave me half an hour of his time in a
busy working week. He said how sorry he and his
colleagues were that they had been unable to save
Joan. He confessed to being baffled about the underlying cause of her illness but said that his 'best guess'
was that her auto-immune system had turned in on
itself and was unable to perform its proper function.
Why this happens in some people, he said, remains a
mystery. He suggested that even had she survived she
would probably have been severely weakened, with a
reduced quality of life. On behalf of myself and my
family, I thanked him for all that he and his colleagues had done and rose to leave. As I went to
shake his hand he surprisingly put his arms round me
and when I said, chokingly, 'I know where she is,' he
replied, 'Yes, and *she* knows where you are.' I was
moved by his evident care and sincerity.

Later I reflected on his words, 'she knows where
you are.' They triggered a train of thought which
had been travelling around my mind for several days.
How exactly *are* our loved ones present to us when
they seem to be totally absent? There are, I suppose
several ways in which people struggle to come to
terms with this paradox. One, is to say that 'they live
on in our memories of them.' Another is contained

in the words of a poem sometimes used at funerals which begins, 'I did not die', and goes on to locate presence in the wind, the rain the snowflake. Or the quotation sent to Sheila Hancock by a friend which ends: 'Listen for my footfall in your heart. I am not gone but merely walk within you.' I could relate to that. More than once, in quite ordinary ways, I experienced that sense of, 'this is the way Joan would have seen it … this is how she would have done it.'

But although there is some value in all these responses they fall short of the full-blooded affirmation of orthodox Christian faith and are ultimately unsatisfying. Certainly, for me they are not enough. 'I believe in the resurrection of the body …' Not this body of flesh and blood but the essential *personality*, the real me. When Christ met his friends in the days following his resurrection, it was *recognisably him*. The same Jesus, who had shared life, love, laughter and tears with them. There was continuity. To say that we live on in the memory of our loved ones, or that having become one with them they walk within us, and then give the impression that this is the *whole truth* about the Christian view of immortality is misleading. It is also, by and large, untrue. How many, for instance remember their great-grandparents?

One day in late April I was browsing in the secondhand section of the SPCK bookshop in

Worcester, when my eye caught a small volume which rang a bell. It was entitled, *A Severe Mercy*. I had a vague recollection of a story involving C. S. Lewis, and a bereavement. On an impulse I bought the book for 50p. It was one of those small incidents which was to be significant and provide an important clue to what was happening in my life. Once I started reading I couldn't put the book down.

Briefly, it tells the story of a young American academic, Sheldon Vanauken, and his wife, Jean, who had met and fallen deeply in love. After their marriage they went to Oxford to pursue research for a year and it was there that they came under the influence of Lewis. When they both became committed Christians they found that they had to review their relationship within the context of their new-found faith in God. On their return to America, Jean contracted cancer and eventually died. A crucial phase of Vanauken's journey through grief involved correspondence with Lewis, who offered bracing consolation: '…from US you have been led back to US and GOD. It remains to go on to GOD and US.' He set this counsel in the context of what he called 'a severe mercy'. Vanauken commented, 'after this severe and splendid letter I loved Lewis like a brother. A brother and father combined.' But it was something Lewis said in a previous letter which caught my attention and seemed to leap out of the page:

It is remarkable (I have experienced it); the sense that the dead person *is*. And also I have felt is *active*; can sometimes do more for you than before – as if God gave them *as a kind of birthday present on arrival, some great blessing to the beloved they have left behind.* (My italics.)

For me, it was one of those 'ah' moments; an important clue to what seemed to be happening to me. How I experienced this I want to relate in the chapters which follow.

5

Surprising Gifts

The communication of the dead is tongued with
fire beyond the language of the living.

T. S. ELIOT, 'Little Gidding'

I'll be seeing you, in all the old familiar places ...

Popular song

☙☙☙

Following retirement from full-time ministry in 2001
I took up (mainly for financial reasons), a part-time
job with the library of University College, Worcester.
In the dark days of January and February this gave
me a reason to get out of bed in the morning, and my
lovely, caring colleagues looked after me with real
sensitivity, encouraging me to talk about Joan, but
also respecting my need at times for space to with-
draw and be on my own.

I don't normally dream much, but one night I
experienced a deep physical need for Joan and eventually fell into a shallow and tearful sleep. This was

followed by the most vivid dream, in which she was
beside me, holding me and talking with me about
ordinary family matters. When I woke up I was
strongly aware of her presence. I wrote in my diary:

> I have no recollection of ever dreaming like this
> before. It seemed totally real. Call it what you
> like, but I have little doubt that it was *her* coming
> to comfort and re-assure me. This was followed
> by a peaceful night's sleep.

I read somewhere that the translation of the Hebrew
in Psalm 127 verse 2, which reads in most versions, 'he
gives to his beloved, sleep', actually means, 'he gives to
his beloved *in* sleep'. Apparently we spend a third of
our lives unconscious. Why then regard that area of
our lives as being outside the touch of God's grace?
Perhaps we need a theology of sleep!

Apart from this, I had no strong sense of her presence, but there were some definite indications that
she was around. C. S. Lewis, in *A Grief Observed*,
which he wrote following the death of his wife, Joy,
spoke of, 'the impression of her mind, facing my
own, an extreme and cheerful intimacy.' As with life's
deepest and most personal experiences it is not easy
to put into words, but for the recipient, the reality is
undeniable and deeply re-assuring.

Over the Christmas and New Year period during
the time immediately before and after Joan's death,

I worshipped regularly at Worcester Cathedral. I wanted to be anonymous, to come and go without having to talk to anyone. On Christmas Day, the Dean spoke of 'this vulnerable fragile baby, the very imprint of God's nature saying, I LOVE YOU, not in order to manipulate, but totally without condition and thereby liberating us.' A fortnight later, the baptismal liturgy contained the promise of God to his people in Isaiah: 'when you pass through the waters I will be with you. I have redeemed you … I call you by name, you are mine.' (Isaiah 43:1–2). Once again the Dean preached, reminding us of our true identity, and that our names are graven on the very hands of God. The following Sunday being the beginning of the week of prayer for Christian unity I decided to go to the Baptist Church. To my surprise, the Dean was the invited preacher! His reflection on the set passage from John 14 spoke powerfully to me, as did the last verse of the closing hymn:

> Green pastures are before me
> Which yet I have not seen
> Bright skies will soon be over me
> Where darkest clouds have been.
> My hope I cannot measure …

So it was, that in those dark days, through this man who was until then only a name, God ministered to me. When I wrote to thank him, I said that it was as if God were putting his arms around me and saying: 'All is well.' I experienced a similar feeling when Luis, a former colleague from Peru, phoned from Lima late one night, having just heard the news of Joan's death, and simply said: 'I am weeping with you.'

There were other gifts too. A book on the stages of grieving co-authored by Evey, a friend from Dorset, with helpful quotes from many sources was a constant reference point. The discovery of a collection of songs by John Bell and the Wild Goose Worship Group, entitled *The Last Journey*, full of bracing comfort and deep understanding helped me considerably, as did two powerful recorded sermons by an Irish-Canadian preacher called Maurice Boyd. I played these recordings again and again.

There *were* lighter moments. Joan and I had discovered Scrabble as missionaries serving in West Africa in the 1960s and played often down the years. One evening in February I had a game with our elder son and his family. I won, which was unusual because when Joan and I played together she invariably emerged the winner! Later that night, lying in bed and thinking of the evening, I found myself laughing aloud, when the thought was suggested, 'You don't think you did that on your own, did you?'!

I confided in a fellow-minister, who was also a widower, 'I really don't think I could face going back to the places which were special to us.' He was thoughtful for a moment then replied, 'Then where will you go? If you are anything like us, you probably did most things together. For me, going back to those places is a kind of communion.' So I decided that over the following three months I *would* visit some of the places where we had lived and worked together.

I returned to Southport to attend the tenth anniversary celebrations of 'Facets', a highly success- ful church-community project, which in its origin and early development had owed much to Joan's vision and imagination. One of my journeys took me to Bakewell in Derbyshire where we had done much of our courting. I walked over the town bridge and up the road, looking for the wooded area where we used to picnic. Inevitably it had changed, much of it having become part of a golf course. As I skirted the edge of the car park, a tall man, about my own age, greeted me and asked if he could be of any help. I suppose I must have looked a bit lost, because when I explained why I was there he was quiet for a moment, then told me that he had just received results of his wife's medical tests, which had indi- cated a terminal illness. He paused, then said, 'Life gets rough doesn't it?' We stood there, total strangers, united in that moment by our shared pain. Walking down the hill I paused to admire the view across the valley and spotted, in the field immediately below me, a hen pheasant followed closely by the brightly coloured male. 'See,' she seemed to be saying, 'they're still at it!'

I travelled to East Anglia, to Hingham in Norfolk, the scene of our first married home, where John, our elder son was born. So many lovely and vivid memories of that scattered rural circuit came crowding back. I went to Norwich, and coming away from the cathedral, was deep in my own thoughts when I heard someone call my name. I looked up. He had recognised me from our college days, though we hadn't seen each other for over forty years. David and his wife Kathy were spending a post-Easter break in the Norwich area. We talked briefly and then exchanged telephone numbers. That seemingly chance meeting was to prove significant. Not only did they open the generous hospitality of their home to me, but David was to become a soul-friend. Vulnerable, he allowed me space to be myself and share some of my deepest feelings. He described himself as a 'wounded healer', and I believe that his coming into my life at that point was an important step in my *own* journey towards healing.

Mid-Wales was a place where we had enjoyed many great holidays. We returned most years to a cottage overlooking the Dovey Estuary kindly made available to us by a doctor friend from one of our former circuits. The family shared our love of 'Cae Top', and I wondered how I would feel, going back so soon after Joan's death. When I parked the car and walked up the drive, the house was empty. On a windless day in early June I sat for about half an hour on the front step, drinking in the quiet beauty of that special place and remembering the good times we had shared. It was, as my friend had said, a kind of communion.

Returning home from Bedford on a sunny Saturday morning, I turned aside, on an impulse, into the village of Sharnbrook, where John had spent a year at the upper school, during our days in the Bedford North circuit. I wandered through the village, and went into the parish church. One of the leaflets which I picked up contained this prayer:

> LORD, where tears fall through tragedy
> or heartbreak, enter the silence and hold me tight,
> lest in bitterness I blame you, or those close to me
> when I should be trusting you with those I love
> and *groping towards gratitude* for the time I have
> been privileged to share with them. (My italics.)

Groping towards gratitude. God's grace mediated through the most unlikely people and in the most unlikely places. Surprising gifts ... but then with the Bible in our hands perhaps we shouldn't be *that* surprised!

6

Taizé

As we enter the third millenium are we sufficiently aware that 2000 years ago, Christ came not to start a new religion but to offer every human being a communion in God? Christ calls us, the poor of the gospel to live out the *hope of a communion, to be a humble leaven of trust and peace within humanity.* (My italics.)

BROTHER ROGER OF TAIZÉ

Ah, Taizé, that little springtime …

POPE JOHN XXIII

ⓔⓔⓔ

A sign that I was beginning to face life again was a returning interest in world affairs. The war in Iraq rumbled on with reports of torture of Iraqis by American and British soldiers and news of daily deaths on all sides. Both Joan and myself had been involved in protests against the war and I had taken part in the huge London march and demonstration in February 2003. I continued to write to my MP about this and issues raised by the deteriorating situation in Palestine.

My diary entry for 9 March reads: 'Taizé material arrived in the post today. I think I will go …' The truth is that I had not planned to go to Taizé. As far back as July 2003 we had booked a week's holiday for the following June in a cottage at Aberdovey. I had decided that although I didn't want to be in Wales on my own that week, it might be good to go away somewhere. I'm not sure how and when, but the idea of going to Taizé was planted in my mind. The two of us had often talked of visiting the ecumenical community in Burgundy which attracts thousands of pilgrims and visitors every year, including many young adults. For various reasons the time had never seemed right, although we had both arranged and attended Taizé-style services down the years. Our interest was renewed during our last appointment in Dorset through a member of our congregation whose own spirituality had been deeply influenced by Taizé and who had been a number of times.

So it was that on a Saturday afternoon in June I stood a little apprehensively outside New Street station in Birmingham, waiting for a bus which would take me on the twenty-hour journey to Taizé. Little did I realise then how much the experience would mean or how great a gift it would prove to be. We

drove through the night, crossing the channel at
Dover and pressing on into the heart of the French
countryside. My travelling companions included a
group of students from Sheffield university and the
Hunt family, Paul, daughter Rosemary from Malvern
and Jane, his sister from Cambridge. They were to
become good friends. I found an almost immediate
rapport with Paul, a retired Anglican priest, who, I
discovered, was like myself a member of
Worcestershire County Cricket Club! We were to
meet a number of times subsequently at New Road.

Arriving at Taizé around 8.30 on Sunday
morning meant that although sound sleep was not
possible, there was time for a wash and some breakfast
before the morning Eucharist in the great Church
of Reconciliation. My first impression was the
makeshift nature of the place, maybe something to
do with the large number of tents clearly visible on
the hillside. Nothing, however could have prepared
me for the experience of sharing in worship with a
couple of thousand people, (many of them young
adults), singing the distinctive chants and songs,
hearing the Scripture read in several languages, and
the SILENCE, which is not perfunctory. It is at the
heart of every service and can last for up to ten
minutes. Receiving communion I found myself very
deeply moved. As the week progressed, I came to
value the three daily services, morning noon and

evening, with little variation in the basic pattern and always that prolonged and profound silence.

I had fully expected that I would be sharing sleeping quarters with at least two other people, and possibly more. As it happened, I was allocated a four-bedded room of which I was the sole occupant. This proved to be a blessing as there were times during the week when I needed to be alone with my own thoughts and feelings.

The crowds of young people in residence that week were mainly from Sweden. The adults had their own morning Bible Study led by one of the brothers, a German, who conducted the sessions in English and German with a simultaneous translation for a small number who heard only French. More than a hint of Pentecost! The small groups which met through the week were truly multi-national. My group included John, an Episcopal priest from Florida, and his wife, Joanne; Eva from Sweden, who spoke little English but wanted to learn more; George, from the Wirral, an optician who had recently come to faith; and Tourbion, a Swedish pastor, whose visiting card contained the words, 'Do as God – become human'! I wrote in my diary:

> Over the course of six days the group changed several times, some leaving and some joining. Yet each time there was a feeling of being

enriched by the newcomers. Here was a 'living parable of fellowship', in which there was no hierarchy, but a deep sharing where each person had a gift to bring and to receive. Language and nationality presented no barrier.

During the previous week, the sixtieth anniversary of the D-day landings had been commemorated. I became friendly with a German about my own age. One day in conversation, it came to us that had we been born a dozen years earlier we might well have been shooting to kill each other on a Normandy beach. It was a reminder of the beginnings of Taizé during the Second World War and Brother Roger's vision of a community of prayer and work with reconciliation at its heart; of how in that tiny almost deserted village he began with his sister to take in Jews fleeing from the Nazi persecution and after the war offered the same hospitality to destitute German soldiers. Gradually other men came to join the community which now numbers over ninety, Protestant and Roman Catholic, from every continent. Some of the brothers work in tough urban and rural situations around the world. Brother Roger, now in his ninetieth year, describes the vision of Taizé as 'a pilgrimage of trust on earth'.

Many memories will remain with me. Attractive Burgundy landscapes, vine-covered hillsides, the

'Source', a tranquil, beautiful place created by the brothers with the theme of water, quiet moments in the village church, touching rosemary outside my window and thinking of Joan, queuing for the simple but adequate food and conversations over meals, evening wine and music at Oyak, a visit to Cluny, which ended in a bar, watching England beat Switzerland in the European Cup(!), young people streaming forward to receive Brother Roger's blessing in the evening service, the creative spirituality of the brothers, and above all, the communal worship. I wrote in my diary at the end of the week: 'Something God has been teaching me here: a deeper trust in himself and in the truth of Mother Julian's words, "all shall be well, and all manner of thing shall be well and all shall be well."'

One of the songs which imprinted itself on my mind and heart is a paraphrase of the words of Teresa of Avila:

> *Nada te turbe, nada te espante*
> *Quien a Dios tie ne nada le falta*
> *Nada te turbe nada te espante*
> *Solo Dios basta.*

Nothing can trouble, nothing can frighten,
Those who seek God shall never go wanting.
Nothing can trouble, nothing can frighten,
God alone fills us.

I left Taizé strengthened and encouraged. I felt sure that it had not only been good for me to be there, but was somehow part of God's unfolding purpose.

7

Exciting Frontier

These things – the beauty, the memory of our
own past – are good images of what we really
desire; but if they are mistaken for the thing
itself they turn into dumb idols, breaking the
hearts of the worshippers. For they are not the
thing itself; they are only the scent of a flower
we have not found, the echo of a tune we have
not heard, news from a country we have never
visited.

C. S. LEWIS

☙☙☙

I recall Professor Cecil Pawson, a former Vice-
President of the Methodist Church, addressing the
Conference as an elderly man and speaking of
approaching 'that *exciting frontier* between death and
what lies beyond'. It is a phrase that has stayed with
me down the years. Inevitably, I have found myself
thinking more than usual about that frontier during
these past months. Words which I have often used in

funeral services now resonate for me with fresh
meaning: words about the distant heaven becoming
'a *home to our hearts*', and the prayer which reminds us
that 'you did not lose our loved ones when you gave
them to us and we do not lose them by their return
to you.' I have discovered how true it is, that we do
not lose the ones we really love.

To be honest (and I say this to my shame), I can
count on one hand the number of sermons I have
preached over the years on the subject of life
beyond death. This would not have been so in the
past, I imagine, when mortality rates were high and
untimely death a common experience. Someone has
said that death has become for us the 'dirty little
secret' that sex was to the Victorians. This is obvi-
ously one reason for the neglect of issues relating to
death and the beyond in modern preaching. There
are a number of others. Eternity is a country we
know little about and although there are some who
claim to have inside information of the geography
of that country, there are relatively few hints in
Scripture which would justify such confidence.
There is also the legacy of past experience where
preachers would use hell and its supposed terrors as
a stick to beat people with, drawing clear lines of
demarcation between the 'saved' and the 'damned'.
This is curious in view of the fact that Jesus did
not 'major' on the subject of hell, and most of his

warnings about its perils seem to have been addressed to religious people.

Then the danger of mawkish sentimentality is always present; projecting our desires on to an imagined better future beyond the bright blue sky, we are tempted to make heaven in our own image. The many references in Victorian hymns to heaven as a place of rest would have seemed wholly attractive to people for whom unrelenting repetitive work formed the parameters of daily existence. Negro slaves in America's deep south sang of 'having shoes and walking all over God's heaven', shoes symbolising the comfort of which they could only dream. We should not dismiss all this too readily. May not the hunger for meaning and justice correspond to reality just as the hunger for food is satisfied by bread?

Hugh Kingsmill once said:

> there are times when I feel my mortality – and I believe it. And there are times when feel my immortality. If I believe one why should I not believe the other?

Even if there is little that we can say about the life of heaven with any certainty, may there be clues in our understanding of the nature of God disclosed in and by Jesus?

I believe that in heaven we will *know each other* with a clarity and at a depth, only glimpsed on earth.

Leslie Tizard said:

> It is not enough to know that our loved ones
> may still continue to exist as drops in an ocean
> of Being. Our moral sense as well as our warm
> human feelings, demand that we shall still exist
> as individuals and that we shall be able to recog-
> nise them.

Not that our relationships will be resumed as they
were in this life, but, as mentioned in a previous
chapter, the resurrection appearances of Jesus indi-
cate strongly that there is a continuity of knowing
and being. Thomas More is reported to have said to
his little daughter on the eve of his execution: 'We
will meet merrily in heaven.'

If a major clue to the Being of God is Trinity I
believe that the life of heaven will be the perfection
of all that we mean by *community*. This all-inclusive
community is described vividly in John's vision in
the book of Revelation, where he speaks of the wor-
shipping hosts of heaven, centred on the self-giving
God, drawn from every people and nation and
tribe. For some this is not an entirely comforting
idea if they are in the business of erecting fences.
Where community is conceived as a living together
of like-minded people there are too many exclusion
zones. There, all are included in an incredible diver-
sity. There we will only be at home, I guess if we are

prepared to get on with those who in this life we would probably have taken a great deal of trouble to avoid.

And I believe it will be a place of *growth and creativity*. I have never been able to understand the picture of death as a final cut off point, at which our destiny is sealed leaving no room for further development. This seems to me to be not only a failure of the imagination, but more seriously to impose limits on the grace and mercy of God. Jesus in that oft-quoted passage in John 14 spoke of the journey beyond death in terms of a series of *stages*, which, unfortunately, the Authorised Version translation of *mansion* totally obscures. At the end of the *Narnia Chronicles*, Lewis says of the children: 'Now they were only just beginning the Great Adventure … in which every chapter is better than the one before.' An exciting frontier, indeed.

Of course, there are difficult questions, to which the only honest answer is, in the words of the hymn: 'I cannot tell'. I struggle when I think of the fate of those who seem to have given themselves to evil; not only the more obvious examples, the Hitlers and the Saddams of this world, but those faceless people; the money men, the arms and drug dealers, whose decisions consign millions of men, women and children to a life of oppression, misery and poverty. If I were God I would probably consign *them* to oblivion.

But in my saner moments I know that life is not that simple and that in the face of the vast inequalities of the world few of us are entirely blameless. Those who indifferently pass by on the other side, or turn a blind eye, must take their share of responsibility. Evil can be very banal and ordinary. In the parable of sheep and goats it was those who refused to welcome the stranger, feed the hungry, visit the prisoner, or care for the sick who heard the awful truth that it was God himself they had failed to recognise in the voiceless, vulnerable poor. I can think of no more terrible judgement than to see in the uncompromising light of complete knowledge, not only those who have been harmed by my words and actions, but those whose suffering I have failed to relieve, either through indifference or cowardice. Then, I can only throw myself on the infinite mercy of God, beyond the reach of which not even the most evil and depraved can fall. The cross is an awesome glimpse in time of eternal mercy and compassion. If a Jewish woman, remembering the horrors of a childhood spent in Auschwitz can find a place to forgive her persecutors, how much more, God …?

In the end perhaps only those who exclude themselves, - whose hearts have become so hardened that they cannot respond to grace, - will remain outside. And I do believe that the justice of God means that heaven will be a place of *righting wrongs*, that justice will not be ultimately denied. That, I take it, is why we pray with Jesus for the Kingdom to come on earth *as it is in heaven*, then roll up our sleeves and work with him to make the dream a reality.

The Celts speak of certain locations as being *thin places*. That is, places where the distance between heaven and earth seems wafer-thin. I know that there *are* such places. I have visited some of them. But in a sense that is true of all places if we had eyes to see and ears to hear. Jacob's ladder pitched between heaven and Charing Cross, is a way of saying that it is only us – our estranged faces – who miss the many-splendoured thing.

Why do we settle for the lowest common denominator in describing the life of heaven? Why is it so often projected as a rather dull state, with endless repetition of the same? Why does it seem so difficult to believe, that if this world is so wonderful and exciting, the world to come must be even more so? Is the idea of the playfulness of God who dances in creation, and heaven as a place of fun and laughter alien to some, because their religion has been so permeated by guilt and so devoid of joy that they have rarely if ever allowed themselves to be overwhelmed by the abundant extravagant grace of God?

Recently someone lent me a novel by Alice Sebold, called *The Lovely Bones*. The story is told by Susie, a girl who having been raped and murdered, goes to heaven, and influences her family from beyond death. Towards the end of the book, there is this description of heaven:

> I would like to tell you it is beautiful here, that I am and you will be, one day forever safe. But this heaven is not about safety, just as in its graciousness it isn't about gritty reality. WE HAVE FUN. We do things that leave humans stumped and grateful; like Buckley's [her young brother] garden coming up one year, all of its crazy jumble of plants blooming all at once. I did that for my mother ... now I am in this place I call this wide, wide heaven because it includes all my simplest desires but also the most humble and grand. The word my grandfather uses is *comfort*. So, there are cakes and pillows and colours galore, but underneath the most obvious patch-work quilt are places like a quiet room where you can go and hold someone's hand and not have to say anything. Give no story. Make no claim. Where you can live at the edge of your skin for as long as you wish. This wide, wide heaven is about flat-head nails and the soft down of new leaves; wild roller-coaster rides and escaped marbles that fall, then hang, then take you somewhere you could never have imagined in your small-heaven dreams.

Of one thing I *am* sure. The commerce of heaven is transacted in the currency of love. Where God, whose nature and name is love, lives and reigns only love will thrive.

> Now we see in a mirror dimly but then face to face; now I know in part ... then I shall understand just as I have been fully understood. Faith hope and love remain ... and the greatest of these is love.
>
> *1 Corinthians 13:13*

8

MOVING ON

The final perseverance of the saints is made up
of ever new beginnings.

ALEXANDER WHYTE

One more step along the world I go …
And its from the old I travel to the new,
Keep me travelling along with you.

SYDNEY CARTER

ⓔⓔⓔ

23 July
County Cricket Ground, New Road, Worcester. The
County is playing Middlesex. Days spent at New
Road this summer have been therapeutic in a way
that only cricket lovers can properly appreciate.
Today there was an odd sense of *dèja-vu*. When
Middlesex began their innings, Hutton and Compton
were batting together! Ben Hutton is grandson of
Len, and Nick Compton grandson of Denis – two of
the finest batsmen ever to play for England. My mind
went back to a day almost exactly fifty years ago

when Denis made a brilliant 94 against Pakistan at
Old Trafford, Manchester. The innings is imprinted
indelibly on my memory. I see as if it were yesterday
the flowing cover-drives, delicate late-cuts and that
characteristic sweep to leg as the ball sped to all parts
of the ground.

Anniversaries

On 18 August we would have been married for forty-
two years. I can't say that I was looking forward to it
and wondered how I should spend the day. In the
end the matter was settled for me. My elder son and
his family had booked a week's holiday in mid-Wales
and asked if I could look after their dog. I stayed
in their home and this turned out to be an ideal
solution. I didn't particularly want human company,
but Lottie is an affectionate animal and Joan was
fond of her.

I planned the day in some detail. After breakfast I
sat down and, imagining that Joan had simply gone
away for an extended vacation, wrote a long letter to
her, describing my days and how I was coping. I told
her how sorry I was for the times I had failed her and
how much I loved and missed her. Looking back it
seems a strange thing to have done but I found it
deeply comforting.

We were married late morning in Belfast and
around 11 o'clock I made my way to the oak tree

which we had planted earlier in the year and quietly
recalled as we always did, the events of that memorable day. The words of the hymn we chose by
Charles Wesley came readily to mind:

> Didst thou not make us one
> That we might one remain?
> Together travel on
> And share our joy and pain.

Normally, we would go out for a meal and I had earlier identified a nearby pub/restaurant with a good
lunch menu. I drank to her, remembering some of
the happy anniversaries we had celebrated over the
years. I spent the afternoon pleasantly in Lichfield,
did some essential shopping and ended up in a tea
room. I was back home by 5.30 and after taking the
dog for a long walk, I spent the rest of the evening
quietly reading and watching TV. I wrote in my diary:
'A day which part of me was dreading turned out far
better than I could have imagined ... another small
but important step in the healing process. I am truly
grateful.'

ⓔⓔⓔ

We had never talked much about our funerals, or
arrangements for the disposal of our remains. However, soon after Joan's death, it came to me quite

strongly that scattering her ashes on the Hebridean island of Iona was something of which she would have approved. But how would the family feel about it? It seemed a long distance to travel, especially with a six-month-old baby. I needn't have worried. From the beginning they were all warmly supportive of the idea so we decided to make it part of a family holiday on Mull in late August.

Joan loved Iona. We had spent part of our Silver Wedding celebration on the island in 1987, and in 1993, as part of my sabbatical, we worked as volunteers for six weeks in the Abbey. We had returned on several occasions, taking groups from our churches to spend a week, living communally with the resident members of staff – often a life-changing experience. We had both become associate members of the Iona Community. For Joan, Iona was not only a place of wild beauty and historic significance, but the focal point of spiritual renewal which she had discovered in the Celtic vision.

We drove across Mull on a cloudy morning from the holiday cottage we had rented at Dervaig for the week. Dwin and Ruth Capstick, former colleagues from our Sierra Leone days and now retired on Mull, close to the Iona ferry, kindly gave us lunch, then accompanied us on the short crossing to the island. Light rain was falling but as we walked up the jetty the clouds blew over, giving way to blue sky and warm sunshine. We made our way to a sheltered beach below the Abbey where Joan used to go to find quietness. Here, Dwin conducted a short, beautiful service and I scattered her ashes in the sea together with a sprig of heather sent by a friend. I thought how thrilled she would be that her children and grandchildren had come together to remember her in this unique place which was so special to her. It was an unforgettable moment.

Into the freedom of wind and sunshine,
> we let you go.
Into the dance of the stars and the planets,
> we let you go.
Into the wind's breath and the hands of the star-maker,
> we let you go.
We love you, we miss you, we want you to be happy –
> go safely, go dancing, go running home.

> Deep peace of the running wave to you.
> Deep peace of the flowing air to you.
> Deep peace of the quiet earth to you.
> Deep peace of the shining stars to you.
> Deep peace of the Son of Peace to you.
> Amen.

@@@

One Sunday morning, some weeks before I retired, I was standing at the door of the church in Gillingham greeting the folk as they left. I had preached on pilgrimage, and the importance of taking the next steps. One member of the congregation said as we shook hands: 'It's time to move on.' If I hadn't known her well, I would have thought she was trying to tell me something! Best part of a year before, her husband had died suddenly and she had gone through a difficult time. Now she was saying that she was ready to take the next steps. There are various stages in moving through the experience of grief, and they will be different for each person. The disposal of clothes and personal effects; first anniversaries; decisions about the future.

One Saturday in March, I was leafing through the *Guardian* magazine supplement when my eye caught the words, 'Let's move to Lichfield'. Although I had made no immediate plans to change my address, the family had suggested that it would be good to move nearer to them (they are both resident in the Birmingham area), and the more I thought about it, the more sensible it seemed. Why wait? So, the following week, I set the wheels in motion, informing the Housing Society of my decision and contacting various estate agents in Lichfield. I didn't expect anything to happen too quickly, but by June I had identified a property which on paper seemed to meet my requirements, an impression which was confirmed on inspection. Within days, the Society had made an offer for 50 Wolsey Road, which was subsequently accepted. Everything was set fair for a move to Lichfield before the end of the year.

Although we had only lived in Worcester for two-and-a-half years, we had put a lot of ourselves, as well as a large proportion of our financial resources, into our retirement home. Living in manses for all our married life, meant that for the first time we had a house we could call our own. Joan was in her element as we chose decor, carpets, kitchen and bathroom fittings, and re-designed the garden. It was almost a complete 'makeover'! As I thought about the move, I felt that I would like to take something with me from the house to be part of my new home in Lichfield. We had always wanted a living-flame fire, and before we left our appointment in Dorset had gone to a showroom in Salisbury, where we had not only chosen the fire, but the surround; we actually watched them cut the marble to size in the workshop. It was then delivered to us and carried in the removal van to Worcester, where it was fitted on arrival. I decided that I would take this fire and surround with me, and when it became clear that there would be logistical problems not only in removing it from Worcester, but installing it in the Lichfield house, I became all the more determined, that however difficult the fire was going with me! When the Housing Society raised objections, it only stiffened my resolve. It became quite literally an obsession. One Monday morning having spent a frustrating hour with a showroom manager in Worcester who seemed intent on persuading me to abandon my plans, I came home, feeling that I had met a blank wall.

What happened next, I still find difficult to explain. If the story had been related by someone else, or I had read it in a book, I would have been sceptical, citing exaggeration or possible coincidence. All I can do is simply relate the incident *exactly* as it happened and leave you, dear reader, to judge.

I had finished lunch and for some reason wanted to listen to a tape by a certain recording artist. I searched high and low for some time but failed to find it. However, I found another box ostensibly containing an album by the same artist. I put it in the machine and switched on.

The tape appeared to be blank. By this time I was annoyed, thinking that I had deleted the contents by mistake. This really wasn't my day! I fast forwarded and turned the tape over. Suddenly, I heard Joan's voice! It was her lost relaxation tape, which had somehow found its way into the wrong box. I dissolved into tears, but kept listening. It was *what* she was saying that held me. She had a gift for visualisation and in her talk, imagined someone walking along a beach, picking up pebbles and stones as he went along. But the stones were weighing him down and he reached a point along the beach where the shoreline became steeper. Deliberately he stopped and taking the stones from his pockets, one by one, made a cairn with them on the sand, and, thus lightened, walked on. It was as if she were saying to me: 'You must leave this obsession behind. It is symptomatic of something else. Lay it down. You are about to make a new beginning.' After that, I didn't give another thought to the fire!

Leaving behind can be painful but it is necessary if we are to move on. Carrying too much excess baggage can weigh us down. The first word God spoke to Abram before he moved out from Ur of the Caldees to make a new beginning for the People of God, was, 'Leave'. One of Joan's favourite hymns which we sang at her Thanksgiving service was composed by Sydney Carter for school leavers on the threshold of a new beginning:

> It's from the *old* I travel to the *new*
> Keep me travelling along with you.

9

Epiphany

The year begins to die.
The year which began with a death.
The new year will be born
out of the ashes of the old.
Just as her death
is the door to rebirth.

☙☙☙

This set down
This: were we led all that way for
Birth or Death?

T. S. ELIOT, 'Journey of the Magi'

☙☙☙

I moved to Lichfield on St Andrews Day. Leaving
Worcester was more emotional than I could have
imagined, mainly perhaps because it was the last
home where we had lived together and reflected so
much of Joan's creative touch. However, about a

week after the move I returned to Lichfield from a long journey and it felt like coming home. A good sign.

I looked forward to Christmas with little enthusiasm. I had sent my Advent letter out early including change of address cards so there was little left to do. Joan had always enjoyed Christmas and the traditions that go with it. At home she would organise the decorations, including a different feature each year. She spent hours on this exercise and the result was both effective and attractive. My main contribution was to help with putting up the tree and making appreciative comments from time to time. Otherwise I kept out of the way and let her get on with it!

So, now, as I hung the cards and dressed the tree I imagined her prompting me and yes, it was a kind of communion. I spent Christmas with the boys and their families. They were feeling Mum's absence too and we looked after one another.

Epiphany
The manifestation of Christ to the nations. When Joan was alive we always kept Epiphany. After the hustle and bustle of Christmas, we felt that folk were ready for a party by 6 January and we would often have a group round for readings, carols, games and food. Joan usually organised these occasions. We

liked to think that as we were concluding *our* Christmas celebrations another branch of the Christian family was just beginning theirs.

Soon after moving to Lichfield, the thought of having a housewarming at Epiphany came to me, but initially I rejected the idea. It seemed too close to the first anniversary of Joan's death. But the more I thought about it the more convinced I became that it was the right thing to do, so I sent the invitations, and began to make plans. It turned out to be a lovely evening, with most of the family present. After the food, I shared a story which we often included in our Epiphany gatherings. The writer of the hymn 'Wise men seeking Jesus' was a Methodist minister called James East who lived in Kettering. He cherished a life-long ambition to visit the Holy Land and had saved for many years to that end. When, around Christmas one year, he checked his savings account and realised that he had just about enough saved for this holiday of a lifetime he made plans to put down a deposit with a view to travelling the following year. About that time he learned that a good friend was seriously ill and in the days before the NHS would need an expensive operation if he were to recover. East realised that the amount of money in his bank account would just about meet the cost of that life-saving operation. His decision was difficult but simple. He withdrew the money, paid for the operation, his friend recovered but he never did make the longed-for trip to Palestine. However, he made a greater discovery which is revealed in the hymn:

> But if we desire him
> He is close at hand
> *For our native country*
> *Is our holy land.*

I was also able to share some good news which arrived just after Christmas. Over £1100 had been donated in memory of Joan for the vital work of re-habilitation in the war-torn West African state of Sierra Leone where we had lived and worked in the early years of our marriage. As a family we had asked that this money be used to purchase an essential piece of equipment for Segbwema Methodist Hospital, now rebuilding after the years of war. I had received a letter from Dr Jennifer Gibson who was working at the hospital over Christmas and New Year, to say that the equipment had arrived and had been used only the day before to treat a sick child. Needless to say, everyone was thrilled and it set the seal on a memorable occasion. We concluded the evening with some lively games!

The next morning marked the first anniversary of Joan's death. Can it really be twelve months since she left us? I had written on 6 January that year, 'I could wish for an epiphany to be given to the men in white coats in this unit. Who knows? This week it may happen.' Now as I stood with John by the oak tree in Sutton crematorium, I recalled the desolation and despair of the days following her death and the gradual emerging from the darkness. Already snow-drops were defiantly braving the winter, not yet half-way over. Later, in the evening as I lit a candle and remembered, the tears which flowed were tears not just of grief but of gratitude. There was much, I felt, to be thankful for.

Epilogue

Tears may linger at nightfall,
but joy comes in the morning.

Psalm 30:5

℮℮℮

Early in January a card arrived from Pearl, who had been a good friend of Joan's during our Dorset days. On the front was a picture of a wood in autumn with a leaf-covered path seemingly petering out among the surrounding trees. The caption read: 'If the path be beautiful do not ask where it leads.' It was a timely reminder not to rush into anything too soon. Yet I sensed in myself a certain restlessness; sure as I was that the way would unfold, I was nevertheless eagerly wanting to move forward into whatever future lay ahead. Of one thing I was sure; the importance of taking into that future the experience of the past twelve months.

So what have I learned over this year? The paramount need to move from fear to TRUST. A strong reliance on God and his loving purposes, which knows that I can entrust the ultimate issues to him and get on with the business of living. This does not mean ceasing to question but the questioning is that of a child who fundamentally trusts the parent. I have learned too, that there is no way to by-pass the grieving process. There were some terrible days when I didn't want to go on. I have done most of my crying in private, around my family and with one or two close friends.

A favourite love song at a concert brings the pain flooding back. Ambushed by tears. But this is part of the healing, and although pain is easing I know there will be more tears to come. I have discovered that this deep, dark valley can be a place of growth, and a point of learning again to hope. Now, it is just possible to sing of 'green pastures and bright skies' without the words sticking in my throat.

And that sense of being 'strangely and wonderfully touched by grace'; a table spread in the wilderness; unexpected gifts and blessings, some of which I have described in this book; intimations of a presence; the feeling at times of being 'prompted'; the indefinable moments when the life of heaven seemed to break through, like a shaft of sunlight surprisingly piercing thick cloud.

Easter on Iona. Unseasonal warmth. Newborn lambs in the fields. Deeply moving liturgies. Stations of the Cross on Good Friday from Martyrs Bay to the Abbey. The terrible emptiness of Holy Saturday.

Midnight vigil, culminating in the triumphant shout: 'He is risen!'

During Eucharistic worship in the Abbey Church on Easter morning, in that part of the liturgy which celebrates our fellowship with the saints, I was invited to speak Joan's name. In the final act of commissioning that evening, the words of Jesus to Peter on the Galilean beach found me with fresh meaning: 'Do you love ME ... more than all else? Feed my sheep ... tend my lambs ... Follow ME!' A call not simply to move on but to recognise Christ's call to present and future ministry.

Twice, during this short period on Iona I visited the beach where we had scattered Joan's ashes. Without being fully aware of it, I realised that I had subconsciously come to Iona, partly at least, to be near to her. Now, I sensed that the words of Jesus to Mary in the garden, 'Don't cling to me,' were being gently but firmly impressed on my mind and heart.

On Monday morning it was cloudy as I made my way to that other beach on the opposite side of the island, which is called Columba's Bay, the place where the saint is reputed to have landed with his twelve followers, before heading inland to establish his monastic mission base. The bay of the back turned to Ireland. So named because there he symbolically left his past behind to make that significant new beginning for Christ and the Kingdom. Is this a major reason why Iona draws people back again and again? Here is the authentic reality of life's rhythms and the truth of the gospel. Leaving to arrive. Losing to find. Dying to live. As I threw my pebble into the sea to symbolise my own leaving, and carried another to a nearby cairn to mark a new beginning, I recalled Joan's meditation about picking up stones and laying them down … the truth I was so slow to learn. I felt lighter, in spite of the rain which was now falling quite heavily. Making my way inland, the words of a prayer which was given to me on the day of her death came to mind:

> Help me to accept that all of life is only on loan to me;
> To believe beyond this present moment;
> To accept your courage when mine fails;
> To recognise the pilgrim of my heart;
> To hold all life with open hands.